GORDON JACOB

HOW TO READ
A SCORE

$1.50

BOOSEY & HAWKES

S Bk. 123   Printed in U.S.A.

PREFACE

THIS little book has been written in the hope that it may be a help to the ever-growing number of those whose enthusiasm for orchestral music has led them to acquire miniature scores of their favourite works. It does not pretend to be exhaustive or to say anything new, but if it helps still further to stimulate such enthusiasm and to elucidate some of the points which usually puzzle the beginner it will have done what it sets out to do.

Though primarily written for amateurs, it may also, the author hopes, be found useful to the general music student who does not specialise in composition and orchestration, but wishes to acquire a working knowledge of score-reading and kindred subjects.

I wish to express my thanks to Mr. Erwin Stein for various suggestions in regard to the musical references.

G. J.
Ewell, 1944.

CHAPTER I. THE FULL SCORE.

A SCORE is, according to the dictionary definition " the original draft, or its transcript, of a musical composition, with the parts for all the voices and instruments ". The word is derived quite simply from the lines " scored " across and down the page. In the course of time this strict definition of a score has been modified so that we now speak of " short scores ", " vocal scores ", " piano scores " and so on when referring to reductions and transcriptions, the original score in which every vocal or instrumental part appears separately being known as the " full score ".

Another word which has come to be used loosely is the word " music " itself. In some quarters it seems, in some unaccountable way, to have become exclusively associated with the piano, " music " and " singing " being rather cynically differentiated. For instance, surprise is sometimes expressed by candidates for admission to the Royal College of Music on finding that all branches of the art including singing are taught there, and not only the piano. But the word " music " is used loosely in another way by professionals as well as amateurs to denote the written or printed copy of a piece of music. Thus we speak of musicians playing or singing " with or without music " (an expression which again might seem to bear a cynical interpretation !) and in the days when music was performed by amateurs in each other's houses we were invited to " bring our music with us " and we modestly " left our music in the hall ", producing it with a great show of reluctance when the longed-for moment arrived. In actual fact Music only exists as sound, the copy is nothing but a graph or blue-print of it. It is for performers to interpret these signs and by their art to translate them into living music.

Up to about the middle of the eighteenth century the standardised orchestra did not exist. Composers wrote their scores with a view to local performance under their own direction and were therefore limited to the instruments which were likely to be available, the composer directing the performance from the harpsichord or organ upon which he gave support and solidity, reading from a kind of musical shorthand which consisted of the bass line provided with figures indicating the harmony. But in the course of time

7

this rather haphazard method was superseded by a more exact one, the figured bass was discarded and the constitution of the orchestra became by degrees more regularised. This gradual standardisation was the result of the work of many composers, chief among them being Stamitz and Gossec, whose music in itself was not of sufficient interest to survive but whose labours paved the way for Haydn and Mozart. With these two masters modern orchestral music may be said to have its origin, for with them the fundamental structure of the orchestra as we know it with its fourfold ingredients of Woodwind, Brass, Percussion and Strings became established.

In illustration of this let us compare the orchestras used by Mozart in the Jupiter Symphony and Strauss in " Ein Heldenleben " :

	Jupiter Symphony.	*Ein Heldenleben.*
WOODWIND.	1 Flute.	Piccolo.
		3 Flutes.
	2 Oboes.	3 Oboes.
		Cor Anglais.
		Clarinet in E flat.
		2 Clarinets in B flat.
		Bass Clarinet.
	2 Bassoons.	3 Bassoons.
		Double Bassoon.
BRASS.	2 Horns.	8 Horns.
	2 Trumpets.	5 Trumpets.
		3 Trombones.
		Tenor Tuba.
		Bass Tuba.
PERCUSSION.	Timpani.	Timpani.
		Bass Drum.
		Cymbals.
		Side Drum.
		Tenor Drum.
STRINGS.		(2 Harps).
	1st Violins.	1st Violins.
	2nd Violins.	2nd Violins.
	Violas.	Violas.
	Violoncellos.	Violoncellos.
	Double Basses.	Double Basses.

(Strauss's harps are put in brackets because though they are undoubtedly stringed instruments they do not belong to the family of bowed instruments and indeed fall under no classification.)

We thus see that despite Mozart's very modest specification, his orchestra can be classified into the same basic groups as Strauss's enormously swollen apparatus.

From a historical point of view it is interesting to note that only a little more than a century divides these two works, the " Jupiter " score having been written in 1788 and " Ein Heldenleben " in 1898.

The absence of clarinets from Mozart's score will be noticed. The reason for this is that, though clarinets are said to have been used by Rameau in 1751 and by Mozart himself in his " Paris " Symphony in 1770, the clarinet was still a newcomer. Haydn used it in some of his later symphonies but it remained for Mozart to discover its possibilities in the orchestra. It is in his operas that it really comes into its own, and Mozart showed also in his clarinet concerto and quintet for clarinet and string quartet that he had quickly realised the capabilities of the new instrument.

There are also no Trombones in Mozart's score. Though the trombone is an ancient instrument it was not used in symphonies before Beethoven's time though Mozart and Haydn used trombones in operas and choral works. Beethoven himself only used trombones in three of his nine symphonies and then very sparingly. They are to be found in the last movement of the Fifth, in the Storm and Finale of the Sixth (Pastoral) and in the Scherzo and Finale of the Ninth. After this, three trombones came to be regarded as normal in the orchestra though Mendelssohn omitted them from most of his purely orchestral works.

With regard to " Ein Heldenleben ", it must not be thought for one instant that an orchestra of this size is normal to-day, indeed the tendency now is towards economy of means. The normal full orchestra consists of the following instruments :

2 *Flutes* (*3rd Flute and Piccolo*), 2 *Oboes* (*Cor Anglais*), 2 *Clarinets* (*Bass Clarinet*), 2 *Bassoons* (*Double Bassoon*).

4 *Horns*, 2 *or* 3 *Trumpets*, 3 *Trombones*, *Tuba.*

Timpani, Percussion (*one or two players*), *Harp, Strings.*

The instruments placed between brackets are either played by a third player or, especially in the case of the piccolo and cor anglais, by the second player if only duple woodwind are used.

The parts for these instruments appear in the score in the order, from top to bottom, as given in the lists above. Thus, with one exception, that of the horns, they are arranged in their groups in order of pitch, the highest at the top of each group. The horns are placed above the trumpets because they are more often used as adjuncts to the woodwind department than as part of the brass though they are, of course, purely brass instruments.

Some composers, such as Wagner, have gone so far as to place the horn parts above the bassoons and the cor anglais below the clarinets because of the frequent blending of these instruments with each other. In old scores the lesser used instruments were placed at the head of the score so that the parts of those most consistently employed should be near together. Thus we find Timpani at the top of the score followed by Trumpets and Horns and below these the woodwind and strings in their normal order. But such things need not detain us now as modern editions all conform to the standard type.

When a work contains a part for a solo instrument, as in a concerto, the solo part is placed above the Strings. Formerly it was the practice to place solo or choral vocal parts between the violas and violoncellos (a relic of the days when the figured bass was read from the lowest line of the score, and the player of it needed to have the vocal parts also under his eye), but nowadays such parts will usually be found above the strings. So much for the lay-out of the score. We will now consider in the following two chapters the two chief difficulties in the actual reading of the score, namely the unfamiliar clefs used for certain instruments and the mysteries of the transposing instruments.

CHAPTER II. CLEFS.

Just as the invention of the zero sign enabled the science of mathematics to develop, so the invention of clefs made possible the exact notation of musical pitch. A clef is a sign which fixes the position of a note on the staff and thus fixes the positions of all other notes as well. There are three clefs used in music, two of which have for some time had a fixed position on the stave, though originally they were movable. These two are the treble, or G clef and the bass, or F clef. Every one who reads this book will be familiar with these two and will be able to read fluently in them, but the C clef is less familiar and is somewhat confusing to the beginner. This clef which fixes the position of middle C has retained some degree of mobility. The lines round which its jaws may now close, thereby fixing that line as C, are the middle line of the stave, and the fourth line counting from the bottom. These positions give us what are commonly known as the alto and tenor clefs :—

Alto clef.   *Tenor clef.*

Both are used by certain orchestral instruments whose living spaces, so to speak, have their centres round about the region between the treble and bass staves and whose parts would, if these were used, constantly change from one to the other if leger lines were to be avoided.

There is also another position of the C clef for which the score-reader must be prepared in the course of his explorations, namely that on the bottom line. This is called the Soprano clef.

It used to be employed for vocal soprano parts to differentiate them from the instrumental parts, which used the treble clef. Most modern editions of vocal works, however, now print the soprano parts in the treble clef. It is not used for any orchestral instrument, but even so late a composer as Brahms employed it in his Requiem and other choral works. Brahms was a great clinger to tradition. The only instrument to use the alto clef now is the viola. The tenor clef is used for the high registers of the bassoon and the violoncello, and is the normal clef for the tenor trombone, though some composers use the bass clef for this instrument, while until quite recent times the alto clef was commonly used owing to the existence in former times of an alto trombone which spent all its time in the alto clef. In so comparatively modern a work as Elgar's Enigma Variations the tenor trombone parts are written in the alto clef. These clefs are used to save a multitude of leger lines. The tenor clef is also very occasionally used for high notes in double bass parts. Certain instruments use only one clef, others two or even three if they have a wide compass which would otherwise necessitate the use of many leger lines. The following table shows the position of the instruments with regard to this question of clefs. Instruments of indefinite pitch such as Bass Drum, Triangle, etc., are not included.

Instruments which use only one clef.	Instruments which use two clefs according to the pitch of a passage.	Instruments which use three clefs according to the pitch of a passage.
(a) *Treble clef.* Piccolo, Flute, Oboe, Cor Anglais, Clarinet, Trumpet, Violin, Glockenspiel, Xylophone. (b) *Bass clef.* Bass Trombone, Bass Tuba, Timpani.	(a) *Treble and Bass clefs.* Horn, Harp, Piano, Organ. (b) *Alto and Treble clefs.* Viola. (c) *Tenor and Bass clefs.* Tenor Trombone (sometimes the Alto clef is met with instead of the Tenor).	(a) *Bass, Tenor and Treble clefs.* Violoncello, Bassoon (Treble clef somewhat rare), Double Bass. (Tenor and Treble clefs are both rarely used, the latter only for Harmonics).

As we shall see in the next chapter, composers use two different systems in writing for Bass Clarinet and Tenor Tuba. These instruments therefore use either Treble or Bass clef according to the system used.

Harp and Celesta parts are written on two staves braced together, like those for the piano. For the organ three braced staves are used, one for each manual and one for pedals. Bach sometimes used the C clefs in his organ works, but this is never done now.

A word should be added about the special use in former times of the treble clef in violoncello parts as the reader will probably come across it in certain editions of classical works. According to this old custom all passages in the treble clef in violoncello parts were to be played an octave lower than the written pitch. Thus we get passages like this:

BEETHOVEN, *Quartet Op. 18, No. 2*

Which would be played as follows:

The treble clef was in fact used instead of the tenor clef just as it is nowadays in writing for tenor voice, where the notes are written an octave higher than the pitch at which they are sung. Vocal tenor parts, however, never go into the bass clef and it is this sudden jolt of pitch to the eye at the change of clef in these violoncello parts that makes them seem so queer when first encountered. As used to-day, passages in the treble clef for violoncello are played at the written pitch. As late as Dvorak the old system was used. The context will almost always show at once whether the new or old method is being employed. Owing to improved technique, modern violoncello parts are liable to go much higher than in classical times, so that the use of the treble clef in the old way would not always be a saving of leger lines. Changes of clef in general are avoided unless the part is going to remain high for some little time. Constant jumping about from one clef to the other is far more tiresome than the reaching of a few notes on leger lines.

Learning the C clef.

Various short cuts are sometimes recommended for reading the alto and tenor clefs by referring them to the treble or bass clefs and then transposing. As these methods involve at least two mental processes instead of one and are also an admission of weakness, the writer scorns to bring them to the notice of such a highly intelligent section of the musical public as the readers of this book. Surely if two clefs can be learned at the age of six or so, two more can be mastered easily by an active-minded adult. And mastered they must be if he wishes a score to mean more to his eye, and through it to his mental ear, than just the general shape of an orchestral passage. The best way to become familiar with these clefs is to play from them on the piano or any other instrument every day for a few minutes and to supplement this by writing tunes in them or transcribing passages into them on paper. Soon certain notes, starting of course with middle C, will become fixed in the mind and in a short time the position of all of them will be secured. There is, of course, bound to be some confusion at first between the alto and tenor clef, but if from the beginning the reader says to himself " This is the *viola* part ", the alto clef will after a little while present itself clearly to his mind, while for the tenor clef he must think " this is a violoncello or bassoon or tenor trombone part " and the alto clef will then be dismissed from his consciousness and all confusion will disappear. When the tone of the instruments comes to be associated with the clefs used by them, eye and ear will collaborate and all will be plain sailing. In this connexion a book of exercises called " Preparatory Exercises in Score-reading ", by R. O. Morris and Howard Ferguson (Oxford University Press), is recommended to those who wish to tackle seriously the problems of clefs and transposition, and who can play the piano a little.

CHAPTER III. THE TRANSPOSING INSTRUMENTS.

FOR various reasons which will be explained, parts for certain instruments are written at a pitch higher or lower than that at which they actually sound. The score-reader must therefore be able mentally to transpose these parts to their proper pitch. Such instruments are known as " transposing instruments ", and here follows a list of them :

Piccolo, Double Bassoon, Double Bass, Clarinet and Bass Clarinet, Horn, Trumpet, Cor Anglais, Tenor Tuba, Saxophone and Bass Flute.

The first three of these are easily disposed of and easily read, as their transposition is only that of an octave. The *Piccolo* is a miniature Flute and as the fingering of both Piccolo and Flute is identical and the pitch of the Piccolo is an octave above the flute, it makes it easier for the player and avoids a multitude of leger lines or 8va signs to write its part an octave lower than it really sounds. Therefore Piccolo parts must be imagined as sounding an octave *higher* than they appear.

The *Double Bassoon* has the same fingering as the Bassoon but its pitch is an octave lower. Ease of reading for the player and avoidance of leger lines below the staff are therefore obtained by writing the part an octave higher than it really sounds. Therefore Double Bassoon parts must be imagined as sounding an octave *lower* than they appear.

In old scores the Violoncello and Double Bass parts were written on one staff, and nearly always played together, apparently in unison. The Double Bass was really, however, playing an octave below the Violoncello so that the single line marked " Bassi " was actually being played all the time in octaves. Now that there is more independence between Violoncello and Double Bass parts than formerly, their parts are written on separate staves but the Double Bass part must be imagined as sounding an octave *lower* than it appears.

The Clarinet.

Two Clarinets appear regularly in scores. One is in B flat, the other in A. This being interpreted means that when the note C is played on the B flat clarinet, the note B flat is sounded, and when the note C is played on the A clarinet the note A is sounded. We might put it thus:

The B flat Clarinet is a tone flat. The A Clarinet is a minor third flat. To rectify this the part for the B flat Clarinet is written a tone higher and that for the A Clarinet a minor third higher than the desired note. Thus, if the orchestra is playing in the key of B flat, the B flat Clarinet will be used and it will be playing in the key of C. If the orchestra is playing in the key of A, the A Clarinet will be used and it will be playing in the key of C. The composer chooses the clarinet which will give it the simplest key to play in. Thus if the orchestra is playing in the key of F he will use the B flat Clarinet which will then play in the key of G, also if the orchestra is playing in the key of E flat or A flat he will use the B flat Clarinet which will then play in the keys of F or B flat respectively. If, on the other hand, the orchestra is playing in the key of D or E he will use the A Clarinet, which will then be playing in the keys of F or G respectively.

In short, the B flat Clarinet is used for flat keys and the A clarinet for sharp ones, because such a procedure ensures a simple key-signature for the Clarinet part.

The reason? Obviously, because the technique of the Clarinet becomes more difficult and awkward, the more sharps or flats there are in the key-signature. Indeed, in the early days of the instrument it was quite impossible to play in any but the simplest keys. In classical times yet another Clarinet was used, in C. The part was not transposed. (C on the instrument=true C.) This was used for the key of C itself, as for instance in Beethoven's 1st Symphony. It was also used for the key of G.

As the technique of the Clarinet improved, the C Clarinet, which apparently had a poor tone, was discarded, so that now we have only the Clarinets in B flat and A. The following quotations will help to drive home these transpositions:

Clarinet in B flat

ELGAR, *"Falstaff"*

Sounds

Clarinet in A

TSCHAIKOVSKY, *Symphony No 6 (Pathetic)*

Sounds

For the *Bass Clarinet* two methods of notation are used. The better of these is that which employs the treble clef—better for the player, that is, and therefore better altogether. The transposition is the same as for Clarinets in B flat and A with the addition of an octave, *i.e.* the transposition is of the ninth and tenth instead of the second and third. Two examples will make this clear :

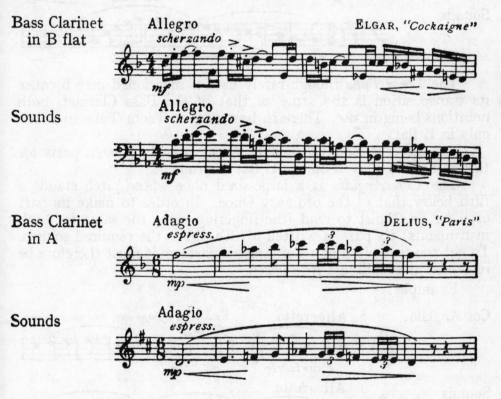

The other method is to write the Bass Clarinet part in the

Bass clef, the transposition being the same as for ordinary Clarinets, for example :

Bass Clarinet
in B flat

Bass Clarinet
in A

Sounds

The *Tenor Tuba* though rarely used is mentioned here because its transposition is the same as that of the Bass Clarinet, both notations being in use. There is, however, no Tenor Tuba in A but only in B flat.

Actually the Bass Clarinet in A has ceased to exist, parts for this being now played on the B flat instrument.

The *Cor Anglais* is a large-sized oboe whose pitch stands a fifth below that of the ordinary Oboe. In order to make its part easy for an Oboist to read (the fingering being the same for both instruments) its part is written a fifth above the required sounds. To get the true pitch of a Cor Anglais passage, it must therefore be imagined as sounding a *fifth lower*.

Example :

Cor Anglais

The Horn.

In classical scores horns in many keys are to be found, namely, C, D, E flat, E, F, G, A, B basso, B flat alto, and B flat basso. In recent times this formidable array has been reduced to one, the Horn in F.

The reason for this welcome change is that up to the forties or thereabouts of the last century the Horn could only play a handful of notes in any given key, whereas since then it has been fitted with valve-mechanism which enables it to play any note within its compass.

Most readers will be familiar with the fact that the notes of a bugle are confined to notes of a common chord based on the bottom note of the instrument, and that these upper notes are harmonics or " upper partials " of that bottom note. The old Horn without valves, or " Natural Horn " as it is called, could produce more of these upper partials than a bugle, but still was very limited in scope. These upper partials, or " open " notes as they are called, are produced entirely by varying the lip-pressure and breathing. Here are the open notes of a Horn whose fundamental note is C :

It follows that a Horn with a fundamental note C would be able to contribute very few notes to a piece in the key of D or B flat, and fewer still in keys like E or A flat. Horn tone was found to be so valuable, sonorous and splendid in the orchestra that something had to be done about it. It would manifestly be absurd to write all orchestral music in the same key for the sake of the horns, therefore the obvious thing was to think of some way of bringing the instrument into line with the various keys. If the length of the horn could be shortened its bottom note (or " fundamental ") would of course be raised and all its upper partials would go up correspondingly, and if it could be lengthened the fundamental and upper partials would be lowered. Accordingly a part of the curved tube of the horn was made detachable, so that bits of different lengths, called " crooks " could be inserted. These crooks were labelled D, E flat, F. etc., to show what fundamental they would produce. But whatever crook he used, the horn player went on calling the fundamental note C and the composer therefore had to go on calling it C too. This gave rise to a system something like the tonic sol-fa in which the key note instead of being called

" doh " was always called C. The composer indicated what **crook** was to be used, the player put it in and went on puffing away **in C** (as he thought) but really produced notes derived from the **fundamental** note whose name was stamped on the crook.

Let us take a simple musical example. Here is a passage which would have been playable on a Natural Horn :

And here are the sounds which would be produced by the **various** crooks :

Remember that for all these the player would be actually *reading* the passage in the key of C.

Horn in C or D
    or E flat, etc.

For easy reference we will take a single note C and show its transposition :

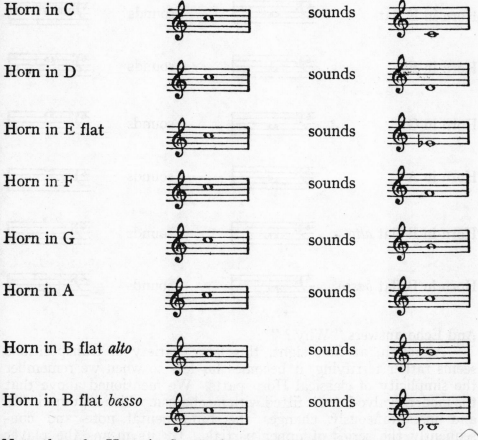

Horn in C	sounds
Horn in D	sounds
Horn in E flat	sounds
Horn in F	sounds
Horn in G	sounds
Horn in A	sounds
Horn in B flat *alto*	sounds
Horn in B flat *basso*	sounds

Note that the Horn in C sounds an octave lower than the written note (just to make it not *quite* straightforward, sighs the reader !)

Before leaving the subject of the Natural Horn, the particular use of the Bass clef must be mentioned. This clef is used for the lowest notes of the instrument, but the transposition is inverted ; for instance the Horn in D transposes up a second instead of down a seventh, the Horn in F transposes up a fourth instead of down a fifth. Thus we have :

Horn in C		sounds	
Horn in D		sounds	
Horn in E flat		sounds	
Horn in F		sounds	
Horn in G		sounds	
Horn in A		sounds	
Horn in B flat *alto*		sounds	
Horn in B flat *basso*		sounds	

And Echo answers " Why ? "

Although, at first sight, this large variety of transpositions seems rather terrifying, it becomes far less so when we remember the simplicity of classical Horn parts. We mentioned above that the modern valve-horn is fitted with mechanism which automatically and instantaneously changes the fundamental note and consequently the series of upper partials. By its means the player opens or closes at will certain sections of tubing instead of having to remove one crook and insert another. He is thus in possession of a Horn which is capable of playing all the semitones between its bottom and top notes. The Horn in F was decided upon as the standard valve horn no doubt because its range was the most useful for filling in middle parts in the orchestral texture. The

Russians were among the first to adopt the Horn in F as the standard, Boródin, Rimsky-Korsakoff, etc., always using it. Since the turn of this century, at least, it may safely be said that all Horn parts have been written for Valve-Horn in F. Exceptions are found in Richard Strauss's works. German composers, notably the traditionalist Brahms, clung to the Natural Horn long after it had been superseded in practice by the Valve-Horn, but Wagner and other go-ahead composers of the nineteenth century soon realised the possibilities of the mechanised Horn. Wagner's writing for Brass is therefore much more modern and advanced than that of Brahms in spite of the latter being of similar or later date. In scores in which the Natural Horn was written for, it was a common practice to write for the two Horns in different keys so as to get a greater variety of notes. Where four horns were used one pair was often in one key and one in another for the same reason, while occasionally all four were in different keys. Thus in Mozart's Symphony in G minor one Horn is in B flat and the other in G in the first and last movements, while in the slow movement, which is in the key of E flat, both Horns are in E flat, and in the Minuet, which has its Trio in G major, both are in G. In Beethoven's Choral Symphony (No. 9 in D minor), four Horns are used, one pair being in D and the other in B flat in the first two movements while in the slow movement which is mostly in the key of B flat, one pair is in E flat and the other in B flat. The last movement starts with one pair in D and the other in B flat, as in the first, but both pairs are in D for the latter part of the last movement when the key becomes firmly D major. Four Horns all in different keys are used by Berlioz. For instance, in " Romeo and Juliet " the work starts with the Horns in E, E flat, G and F respectively, and the crooks are changed fairly frequently throughout the work. This gave him a large selection of notes to play about with, though all four were Natural Horns.

It took time for the Valve-Horn to become firmly established in the orchestra and in scores written during the period of transition we may find one pair of Natural and one pair of Valve-Horns employed. Wagner did this in his early operas, so that in the Tannhauser Overture, for instance, we see one pair of " Waldhörner " (Natural Horns) and one of " Ventilhörner " (Valve-Horns), both pairs in E.

Nowadays all Natural Horn parts are played on the Valve-Horn in F, the player doing the necessary transposition of his part at sight. Many composers also nowadays reject the anomalous notation in the bass clef, the transposition being the same as in the treble clef.

The Trumpet.

Most of the above remarks about the Horn are applicable also to the Trumpet. This instrument too was originally a Natural Trumpet without valves and therefore was fitted with various crooks. As the Trumpet is an octave higher in pitch than the Horn the transposition in some cases is up instead of down, *e.g.*, the sound of the Trumpet in D is a tone above the written note, not a seventh below, that of the Trumpet in E flat is a minor third above instead of a major 6th below, and that of the Trumpets in E and F are respectively up a major third and a perfect fourth. The transposition of the Trumpets in B flat and A is however exactly the same as that of Clarinets in the same keys, while the Trumpet in C sounds the written note, not its octave below. The following shows the transpositions at a glance :

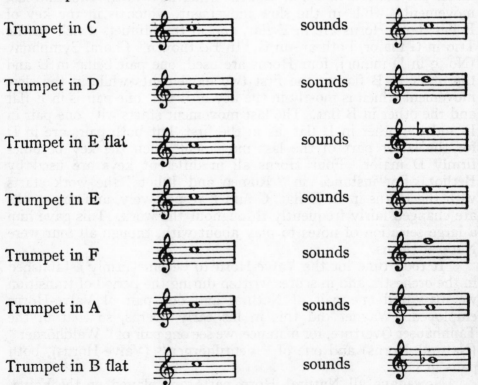

Trumpet in C		sounds
Trumpet in D		sounds
Trumpet in E flat		sounds
Trumpet in E		sounds
Trumpet in F		sounds
Trumpet in A		sounds
Trumpet in B flat		sounds

Trumpets in other keys were also in existence but need not detain us as they were hardly ever used. As on the Natural Horn, crooks were used to change the keys, and the open notes were the same as those of the Natural Horn.

The standard valve-trumpets in use today are those in C, B flat and A. The A Trumpet is however not used much as it is an adaptation of the B flat instrument and is not very well in tune. The C Trumpet is often indicated in modern scores, which saves the reader much trouble in transpositon, but in this country the B flat Trumpet is now used almost exclusively, the player doing any necessary transpositon himself when playing from parts written in other keys. A small Trumpet in D is often used for Bach and Handel parts as those composers generally wrote for the D instrument and their parts usually would lie rather high for the B flat Trumpet.

Before leaving the Horn and Trumpet, a word needs to be said about the process known as " hand-stopping " on the Natural Horn. Sometimes notes are found in parts written for Natural Horn which are not true upper partials. These were obtained by the action of the hand in the bell of the instrument which had the effect of flattening or sharpening the open note. They were of different quality from the open notes, and much inferior, but they did give composers a chance of obtaining more notes than the Natural series of upper partials afforded. On the whole, however, the classical composers confined themselves to the open notes.

Some stopped notes are to be found in the Trio of the Scherzo of Beethoven's 3rd Symphony (Eroica). In this symphony the very rare number of three horns is employed. Stopped notes were not used on the Trumpet. They were difficult to produce, and of very poor quality. The use of stopped notes on the Horn for special effects in modern music will be referred to later in this book.

The Saxophone.

Saxophones are rarely used in the orchestra, but as they sometimes make their appearance they must be mentioned here. There is a whole family of them from Sopranino down to Contrabass. The complete list is as follows :

            Sopranino in E flat (or sometimes in F)
            Soprano in B flat.
            Alto in E flat.
            Tenor in B flat.
            Baritone in E flat.
            Bass in B flat.
            Contrabass in E flat.

And here are their transpositions. The treble clef is used for all of them, by the way :

Suppose the written note  is played by each in turn.

The results in sound would be

Sopranino in E flat   in F

Soprano in B flat

Alto in E flat

Tenor in B flat

Baritone in E flat

Bass in B flat

Contrabass in E flat

The Saxophone usually employed in the orchestra is the **Alto in** E flat, but in Ravel's Bolero there are parts for Sopranino in F, Soprano in B flat, and Tenor in B flat. But it is very exceptional to find Saxophones in orchestral scores at all.

The Bass Flute or Alto Flute.

This is also a great rarity, but parts for it occur in Stravinsky's "Sacre du Printemps" and in such well-known works as Ravel's "Daphnis and Chloe", Vaughan Williams' "Job", and Holst's "Planets". It is in G, and is written a fourth above the sound intended so that its part can be read by an ordinary flautist, the fingering being the same as that of the ordinary flute.

Transposition :

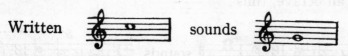

Written [♪] sounds [♪]

For completeness two more rare instruments whose parts transpose must be mentioned, namely the *Clarinet in E flat*, and the *Oboe d'amore*. The Clarinet in E flat transposes like the trumpet in E flat, *i.e.* up a minor third, and the Oboe d'amore like the Clarinet in A, *i.e.* down a minor third. The Clarinet in E flat is common enough in Military Bands which always contain at least one, and Berlioz, Strauss and Elgar have used it in their symphonic works. The Oboe d'amore is an old instrument used in the time of Bach, and recently revived. Parts for it occur in Ravel's " Bolero " and Strauss's " Sinfonia Domestica ".

Turning to instruments other than Wind Instruments, parts for *Celesta, Glockenspiel* and *Xylophone* are written an octave lower than their true pitch. In old scores *Timpani* parts were always written on the notes C and G, the tuning being indicated at the beginning. But now the true sounded notes are always written.

A few aids to Transposition.

Here are a few tips which are quite useful :

(i) The Horn in D may be read in the Alto clef, the proper key-signature being added, thus :

Horns in D [music] sounds [music]

(ii) The Bass Clarinet in B flat and Tenor Tuba in the Treble clef, also the Horn in B flat *basso* may be read in the Tenor clef, thus :

Bass Clarinet in B flat, or Tenor Tuba in B flat, or Horn in B flat basso

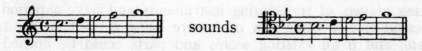

[music] sounds [music]

(iii) The Horns in E flat or E may be read in the Bass clef, **the** proper key-signatures being added and the notes transposed up an octave, thus :

Horns in E flat 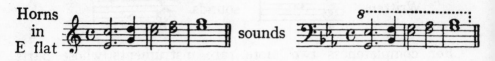 sounds

Horns in E 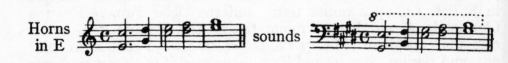 sounds

There are no easy ways of reading Clarinet and Trumpet parts in B flat or A, nor Horns in F. This is unfortunate as these are the transpositions most frequently met with. A little keyboard-work will help here and the Morris-Ferguson book of Exercises recommended above for the clefs will be found of great assistance also in transposing.

It is advisable to get into the habit of transposing mentally from one key into the other rather than laboriously to transpose each note as it comes.

Classical Horn and Trumpet parts are so simple and so rarely employ accidentals that no difficulty should be experienced with them. But Clarinet parts and modern Brass parts are harder to read because they may contain a good many accidentals.

From time to time efforts have been made to rationalise this transposing business by printing scores with all notes at their true, sounding pitch. But as this means that the score is not identical with the parts it is liable to lead to misunderstandings between players and conductor at rehearsals. Also to anyone accustomed to the transpositions the score looks wrong and fails to register its effect automatically on the inner ear. We have seen, too, that the transpositions are based on the technique of the instruments, and this would have to be revolutionised if the rationalised method were to be successfully introduced. If we could kill off all the existing players of transposing instruments and have a period of orchestral silence while new ones were being trained on the new system, and if all existing scores and parts could be burned or repulped and new ones printed, such a revolution might be possible. But you cannot do that sort of thing in democratic countries.

One more point before we leave this subject. We have seen that in the old Natural Horn and Trumpet days the parts for these instruments were always written in C, the crooks regulating the actual pitch. This custom of writing Horn and Trumpet parts without any key-signature has persisted up to the present day, though some composers have been using key-signatures for these parts in recent years. In the majority of scores the reader will find, therefore, no key-signatures for these instruments. This facilitates spotting the parts in the score, but it often results in a great many accidentals.

CHAPTER IV. NOTATION OF PERCUSSION BAND PARTS.

THE Percussion department, or " Kitchen " as it is irreverently called in the profession, consists of all the various Drums, Cymbals, Gong, Triangle, Xylophone, etc., etc. Some of these instruments give notes of definite pitch, and some do not. The most important, and often the only member of this varied assemblage to be found is the Timpani or Kettledrums. In classical days two of these were used, tuned to the two principal notes of the key of the piece, tonic and dominant. Modern scores always demand three, which are tuned to any notes required by the composer, the tuning being changed, often quite frequently, in the course of a piece. In some works in which a very large orchestra is used, two players each with a set of drums may be required but this is comparatively rare. Berlioz used three sets of drums operated by three players in his most remarkable " Symphonie Fantastique " and he made them roll together in three-part chords.* This symphony, by the way, which has been described as the first " modern " orchestral work, was written well over a hundred years ago. Some of it was, in fact, sketched in the year 1827, the year of Beethoven's death. Some modern works are written with " machine-drums " in view. " Machine-drums " can be made to alter their pitch instantaneously by means of mechanism which tightens or loosens the parchment or " head " of the Drum at the player's will. In the absence of Machine-drums such parts may require six or seven ordinary Drums, otherwise the player could not cope with all the rapid changes of pitch required. When ordinary kettledrums, not Machine-drums, are used, the instruction in the score is usually given in Italian. The direction " Muta A in B " means " change A to B ", and must not be confused with the English word mute which in Italian is " sordino ". Suitable time for the screws to be turned has to be allowed by the composer when making these changes.

---

* In his Requiem he used eight pairs of drums and ten players!

The roll is indicated by the ordinary sign for a shake or by a tremolo indication thus :

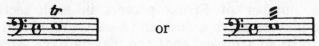

In slow time the second method is rather ambiguous as it might be taken for, and indeed is sometimes intended to be, an indication of repeated demisemiquavers. These two methods are used for all percussion instruments which roll. Timpani parts are written in the Bass clef and sound at the written pitch. Two other sorts of Drums are commonly used in the orchestra, namely the Bass Drum and the Side Drum. These do not give notes of definite pitch but are conventionally written as a rule on the note C, the Bass Drum in the Bass clef in the second space, and the Side Drum in the Treble clef in the third space. Such instruments as the Triangle and Tambourine, which are also of no definite pitch, are similarly written in the Treble clef, but when several of these instruments are used together they are sometimes written on different notes so as to distinguish them from each other. In some scores, in order to save space, when several different percussion instruments are used together, their parts are written not on staves at all but on single lines.

Bass Drum and Cymbal parts are requently written on one staff, as they are often played by one performer. In this case the Bass clef is used, the Bass Drum being as usual in the second space and the Cymbals in the fourth. The Bass Drum notes have their tails down, and the Cymbals up.

Band Parts.

Each instrument has its own part drawn from the score. The numbers of bars during which an instrument is silent are indicated numerically and have to be counted by the player. When a large number of bars' rests are to be counted, cues are given from other parts as a check in case the player gets lost in his counting. It is a tedious business counting rests and it is easy to slip a bar or two. In order to save time at rehearsal, letters are inserted at frequent intervals in the score and parts. These are used as starting-points when stops are made at rehearsal. Sometimes, instead of letters, every tenth bar is numbered. In some cases each pair of instruments shares a desk, the parts being written on two staves braced together on the same sheet. This is rather a help to the players in checking the counting of rests and so on, but quite often each part is written out on separate sheets. As there are a number of String players in each section of the Strings, two players share a desk and a part. Wind and percussion parts have to be so arranged that the players have a rest in which to turn over the page. This is also done if possible in the String parts, but it is not always feasible as the Strings often play continuously for a long time, and as they share parts, one player can turn while the other carries on.

In the case of manuscript works, the parts are copied from the score by a professional copyist who, in addition to having very clear and legible musical handwriting, must also possess sufficient musical intelligence to provide sensible and useful cues and generally to lay out the part in a workmanlike manner. Sometimes he has to be able to decipher very untidy and ill-written scores, but most experienced composers have learned by bitter experience to make their scores tidy and legible. Nothing puts players and conductors off a new work more than constant stops at rehearsal to correct mistakes in the parts. Legibility and clarity of writing are the lubricating oil of the orchestral engine. Some composers are temperamentally unable to write tidily, and their scores never get any better in this respect as long as they live. Thus Beethoven's scores were always terrible to read while Wagner's from first to last were models of calligraphy. It should not be necessary for a composer who really knows his job to make a rough copy first. He should be sufficiently sure of what he wants and how to get it to be able to write a fair copy straight away without any erasures to speak of. Of course he usually makes a rough " short score " first, but of that more anon.

CHAPTER V. SPECIAL EFFECTS.

SPECIAL effects may be defined as sounds obtained by using instruments in some way which differs from the normal in some degree, and which require particular directions to the player.

Special effects on the Strings.

(i) *Con sordino, i.e.* with the mute. Mutes are appliances which when fixed to the bridge of a stringed instrument prevent more than a fraction of the vibration of the strings being transmitted to the body of the instrument and thus reduces its power and muffles its tone. Mutes are now used on all stringed instruments and vary in size from quite a small one for the Violin to a giant for the Double Bass. In classical times mutes were seldom used on the Violoncellos and Double Basses even when the upper Strings were muted. But in the slow movement of Beethoven's Pastoral Symphony two Violoncellos are directed to play with mutes while the rest play with the Double Basses unmuted. None of the upper Strings are muted and one is led to the conclusion that these Violoncello parts sounded too thick and prominent at rehearsal and so it was decided to mute them. In the slow movement of the same composer's " Emperor " Concerto both Violin parts are muted, but not the Violas, Violoncellos and Double Basses. When mutes are put on or taken off during the course of a piece, the composer has to contrive a few bars' rests for the Strings for this purpose. An interesting device is used by Sibelius in " Tapiola " where, at bar 462 he allows three bars for putting on the mute, but at bar 513 he wants the mutes taken off without interrupting the violins. He therefore gives the instruction " poco a poco senza sordini ", which means that each desk ceases playing in turn for long enough to take off the mute. The mute can be taken off a good deal quicker than it is put on, for in addition to searching their pockets for their mutes, the players must fix them firmly to the bridge, which takes a few seconds more than just whipping them off does. Putting mutes on and off in the course of a quiet piece is always inclined to be disturbing to the audience as there is almost always a slight clattering and rustling about in the orchestra which brings the audience back to earth. Even in the best disciplined and most conscientious orchestras this cannot be avoided to some extent.

(ii) *Pizzicato*. This well-known effect is obtained by plucking the string instead of bowing it. The instruction for resuming the bow is *arco*. A well-known movement in which the Strings play pizzicato throughout is the Scherzo of Tschaikowsky's Fourth Symphony. This is an example of pizzicato on a heroic scale. On a less heroic scale but even, we fear, better known is the Pizzicato from Delibes' " Sylvia ". In such movements the bow can be laid down but usually Pizzicato lasts only for a short time in the course of a piece, and alternates with arco, in which case the bow is of course retained throughout.

A very special effect, the Pizzicato tremolo, is used by Elgar in the accompanied cadenza of his Violin Concerto.

(iii) *Col legno* (with the wood). This means that the bow is to be turned over and the strings struck in a bouncing way with the wood of the bow. It is a rare effect but both Berlioz and Wagner employed it. Holst used it in one of his " Rig Veda Hymns ", Saint-Saens in his " Danse Macabre " and Sibelius writes a tremolo col legno in " The Swan of Tuonela " which has an extraordinarily eerie effect (letter H).

(iv) *Sul ponticello*. This is a direction to the player to apply his bow to the string at a point nearer the bridge than is normal. When used " forte " the effect is rather harsh and metallic, but it is usually employed in conjunction with " piano " or " pianissimo " tremolo, which produces a very eerie and mysterious sound productive of goose-flesh in the hearer. The old masters did not use it but it is of fairly frequent occurrence in scores from Tristan onwards. It is usually only employed for a few bars at a time.

(v) *Sul Tasto* or *Sur la touche*, indicates the opposite of ponticello, *i.e.* the bow is drawn across the string further away from the bridge than the normal. Literally it means " on the fingerboard ". This effect, like the ponticello, is usually found in conjunction with soft tremolo and it produces a very light and whispering sound. Ravel uses this indication a great deal in his Rhapsodie Espagnole (1st movement) and it is of fairly common occurrence in modern scores. String players often use it when it is not indicated by the composer in order to produce a fine degree of pianissimo.

(vi) *Harmonics.* This is a technical subject and those who wish to understand it thoroughly should consult textbooks of orchestration. Suffice it to say here that there are two kinds of harmonics on stringed instruments—natural and artificial. The natural harmonics are upper partials of the open strings which are made to vibrate sectionally by lightly touching them at certain fractional (or " Nodal ") points. The notation of these is simple, the note required to be sounded being written at its true pitch with the sign " o " above.

For instance

indicates the second upper partial of the open A string, while

might be obtained as the second partial of the D string or the third of the G. The player uses whichever is most suitable to the context unless the string is indicated by the composer. Artificial harmonics as used in the orchestra are obtained by stopping a note in the usual manner with the first finger and touching it lightly at a point a fourth above with the fourth finger. The stopped note is written as an ordinary note, the touched note as a diamond-shaped white note, thus :

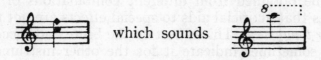

i.e. two octaves above the stopped note.

Both natural and artificial harmonics can be produced on all the stringed instruments except the Double Bass which can only obtain natural harmonics because the stretch of a fourth is too wide for the fingers on one string. Harmonics

35

are used to obtain very high notes of an elusive and very quiet character.

Divisi. Though this does not indicate a special way of playing, it may be mentioned here as a special effect from the orchestral point of view. Ever since the time of Weber composers have from time to time sub-divided their string-group into a number of parts. Divisi or div. a 2 means divide into two parts, div. a 3 into three, and so on. For instance in the Prelude to Lohengrin, Wagner uses four solo violins detached from the main body, while the rest of the violins are divided into four equal parts. Examples of divisi in modern works are legion, but a few specially striking ones may be mentioned, for instance on p. 55 of " The Dream of Gerontius " Elgar divides each string-group into three parts playing held chords of fifteen notes altogether, and in the " Tallis Fantasia " two separate string orchestras as well as a solo quartet are used by Vaughan Williams who obtains by this means many subtle effects, whilst Sibelius in " Tapiola " provides almost throughout the score many varied types of divisi. Indeed, in modern scores, few bars pass without the use of divisi. A very early example is to be seen at the beginning of Mozart's G minor symphony where the Violas are divided into two parts, and an example from Beethoven of divided Violas used in conjunction with Woodwind, and each section playing double stops is to be found in the last movement of the Choral Symphony in the Adagio section in G minor (" Ihr stürzt nieder, Millionen ? "). He used similar colouring in the " Benedictus " of his great Mass in D.

Special effects on Woodwind.

No satisfactory method has been devised for muting Woodwind instruments, though both Berlioz and Rimsky-Korsakoff experimented with the idea of enclosing them in bags made of cloth, without much success. There are indeed such limitless varieties of effects to be obtained from different combinations of Woodwind instruments that artificial aids to special effects are not necessary.

Flutter-tongueing. This is best on the Flute and Piccolo, though composers sometimes indicate it for the other instruments. It is executed by rolling the tongue and is usually associated with rapid chromatic scales or such-like. It is said to have been first used in the orchestra by Richard Strauss for the windmill scene in " Don Quixote ". There is a good deal of it in Stravinsky's " Sacre de Printemps " not only for Flutes.

The writer remembers reading somewhere that Ravel in one

of his works imitates a cock-crow by instructing his Bassoon player to remove the reed from his instrument and blow through it. This effect can often be heard while an orchestra is tuning up.. An Oboe reed sounds very spiteful and bad-tempered indeed !

Special effects on Brass.

The Mute. Horns, Trumpets and Trombones are all frequently muted, and even the Tuba sometimes has to use the mute. The effect of the mute on brass instruments is not only to damp down the sound but also to change the tone-colour. Hence the mute is often used in loud passages as well as soft. Many different sorts of mutes made of different materials and of different shapes are used by Trumpet and Trombone players in dance bands and attempts have been made in recent years to introduce these into the symphony orchestra. But the usual orchestral mute is made of metal and is pear-shaped so as to fit into the " bell " or open end of the instrument. The tone of a brass instrument is stifled and becomes very nasal and prominent when it is blown hard and loudly, while in soft passages it lends a distant and magical colour to the orchestral palette.

A well-known and marvellously realistic example of pictorial music is provided by Strauss in " Don Quixote " where he uses muted brass tongued rapidly to represent a flock of sheep. In the same work he makes a good deal of use of muted tenor and bass Tubas. Most modern works contain examples of muted brass, indeed it is an effect which has been rather overdone in recent years, but it is a great temptation to use it because of its intensely dramatic nature.

Hand-stopping on the Horn. The score-reader will often come across Horn notes with a cross + placed above or below them. This is an indication that the hand is to be pressed well into the bell of the instrument, thus producing the muffling effect of the mute. When blown hard a very rasping effect is produced. The French words " sous bouchés " (" muffled sounds ") or " cuivré " (" brassy ", for loud passages) are often ended. The effect is almost identical with that obtained by the mute, but it can of course be applied instantly, and therefore is very useful for echo effects when soft or for sudden and startling ones when used loud. This effect is impossible on the other brass instruments because of their shape and position with regard to the player's hand.

The Trombone glissando. By pulling in or out the slide a glissando can be obtained on the Trombone. This is not very often used in serious music, because it is apt to make the audience laugh in the wrong place, but at the culminating point of a great climax its tearing effect may be highly effective, *e.g.* the last half-dozen bars of Ravel's " Bolero ". It is used a good deal in dance-bands.

Special effect on the Harp.

Harmonics. The middle strings of the Harp can be induced to give their first harmonic (*i.e.* an octave above the normal note of the string) by touching it at the centre and plucking the upper half. The harmonic sign " o " placed above a note thus indicates that the note sounds an octave higher, *e.g.*

Owing to the position of the hands, chords up to three notes can be played as harmonics by the left hand, but only single notes by the right.

Harp harmonics have an ethereal bell-like quality. The reader will come across them in most modern scores which contain Harp parts.

Special effects on Percussion.

Variety in this department is obtained on the whole by employing different instruments, but sometimes a composer will indicate that Cymbals are to be struck with a wooden or soft-headed stick, that the Side Drum is to be played with loose snares, *i.e.* muffled. Snares are gut strings stretched across the lower head of the Side Drum. Sometimes too the Timpanist is instructed to use hard or soft sticks or even Side Drum sticks, as in Variation XIII of Elgar's " Enigma " Variations. In actual fact, to get the degree of pattering pianissimo required in this Variation, pennies are often used instead of sticks. Occasionally the Timpani are muffled by placing baize on the Drum head. But most of the time percussion players are allowed to play their instruments in the normal way. Mention must be made here of the wire brush sometimes used on the Side Drum instead of sticks, but this belongs properly to the dance-band, though it sometimes finds its way into symphonic scores. A variety of sound effects by various means is obtained in Béla Bartók's Sonata for Two Pianos and Percussion.

CHAPTER VI. AURAL IMAGINATION.
HOW TO MAKE THE BEST USE OF A SCORE.

The ideal to be aimed at is to be able to " see with the ear and hear with the eye ". Musicians vary very much in their powers in this direction. Some indeed go so far as to say that they get more enjoyment out of reading through a score than from hearing the work performed. They profess to be able to hear so minutely and exquisitely with their inner ear that their imaginary performance transcends any actual one that could possibly take place. This is obviously fallacious because the impact of music on the ear causes a physical sensation. One might as well say that the imaginary taste of a glass of champagne is preferable to the real thing or that a hungry man can be satisfied by a " still life " of a beef-steak pudding. Can one imagine sitting in solemn silence poring over a score and feeling the thrill and excitement of a well-built crescendo, the poignancy of a fine-drawn melodic phrase or the sharp stab of a sudden sforzando chord on the Horns ?

These things can certainly be pictured by the inner ear but not really experienced by it. Indeed, the mere taking in by the eye of all the notes on a page *at playing speed* is often a physical impossibility.

And here we must point out the difference between memory and reading. It is certainly possible to recapture to a very large extent the sound of a work which one has heard many times, and the score aids greatly in this, but there is a world of difference between this mental process and the reading of a previously unheard score. Suppose a musician were asked to assess the value of a new work from the score, and suppose the work to be a quickly moving one which plays for five minutes and is scored for a large orchestra. We should not give much weight to such a musician's opinion if after five minutes he closed the score and gave his opinion of it unless, of course, its technical incompetence could be seen at a glance as sometimes happens. No, a new work needs careful study even by the most expert eye before its effect can be gauged at all accurately. The question of " idiom " comes in too. Most musicians could hear almost at playing speed a previously unheard work by Bach, Mozart or Beethoven, or any composer whose style

and mode of musical speech have become familiar by long acquaint-
ance, that is to say the general effect would be got at a first read-
through, but not, especially in the case of Bach, a really detailed
impression of the interplay of the contrapuntal lines. But what of
Bartók, Stravinsky, Schoenberg and Co? Here would occur con-
catenations of notes in unfamiliar juxtapositions, swiftly changing
time-signatures, probably no easily assimilated melodic ideas even.
Little help would be gained here from memory of previous musical
experiences by those only familiar with the classics and even one
well versed in the various techniques of " modernism " would have
to spend much time in study before 'such a score began to yield up
its secrets. For not only is the musical language itself uncomprom-
ising, but the instrumental colouring is quite likely to be new and
original in conception.

How then is the intelligent musical amateur to get the most
value out of his library of miniature scores, and what use is he to
make of them?

He must, of course, start with the simplest classical scores.
Supposing a Haydn Symphony is to be played at a Prom.; he must
contrive to spend some time before the concert with the score,
conscientiously reading all the notes in it and not slurring over the
transpositions and C clefs. If necessary he should try to unravel
any complicated passages on the piano, playing, however slowly,
in time. He must try to imagine the effect of the instrumental
combinations and mark in the score any passages he finds difficult
or impossible to hear mentally. Then comes the concert. The music
flies past his physical ear, his eye and mind are concentrated on
the score, pinning down sounds so that the signs on the paper shall
for ever mean *sounds* to him. After the concert he goes through
the score again, and while the impression is fresh he finds he can
hear much of it in his mind's ear just as it was at the performance.
Each time this is done with real concentration will make the next
effort easier.

" Yes," the reader will say, " that's all very well for music
students, but I've got my work to do and it doesn't leave much
time for all that ". Granted, but what of journeys to and from
work, lunch hours and long winter evenings? Never mind if the
other occupants of the bus or tube view you as a mild lunatic
because you are reading a score instead of the results of the 3.30;
besides, not being a music student, you can afford a gramophone
and plenty of records and this will ease your task enormously, for
instead of one fleeting performance at a concert you can hear a

fine performance under Beecham, Toscanini, Wood, Boult, etc., whenever and as often as you like, following the score each time, and each time seeing and hearing more in it. The gramophone is, in fact, the key to the situation, but do not be a mere passive recipient of what it and the wireless offer. The world's masterpieces are open to you, and in the gramophone you have the complement of your library of miniature scores. Together they will help you to get inside the minds of composers and to see their visions and dream their dreams.

Gradually a full score will come to be to you what it was to the man who made it, a veritable picture of subtle sound-shapes, but one word of warning with regard to the gramophone. Do not let it take the place of the real thing. However good a record may be it cannot be the same as a performance in the flesh. There is a brilliance and clear-cut outline in an actual performance which is lacking in any mechanical reproduction, also the mere sight of an orchestra in action with its rhythmically moving bows, its intense concentration, and its beautiful shining array of instruments is an enormous stimulus to musical enjoyment.

Let it not be thought either that an understanding of technique and the ability to read scores is indispensable to the enjoyment of music. There are many music-lovers of taste who know nothing of these things, yet even a little knowledge adds tremendously to one's appreciation of what is going on and much to the zest of listening.

With regard to the ability to recognise the sound of each instrument, which is of course the first requisite of the score-reader, this can only be acquired by observation. Listening to an orchestra, score in hand, the reader will soon learn to recognise the instruments when he hears them and will thus acquire the power of calling up to his mind's ear the sound of any simple instrumental combination. Such an instrument as the Oboe with its pungent " tang " is easy to recognise, but it needs some practice to be able infallibly to distinguish Flute from Clarinet on certain notes, and softly played Horns from Bassoons. Wind instruments sound very different at different pitches, notably the Clarinet, whose lowest register is hollow and sinister and in complete contrast with its clear and pure tone in the middle and upper registers. The low notes of the Flute are also very characteristic and bear a marked resemblance to the tone of a quietly played Trumpet. Among the brass instruments the Horn is distinguishable from the Trumpet and Trombone by reason of its slightly muffled and veiled quality, and even when

played very loudly it never gives the open-throated and impressively
" brassy " tone of the Trumpet and Trombone. Trumpets and
Trombones are almost identical in timbre, Trumpet tone being an
extension upwards of that of the Trombone or *vice versa*. The
Tuba differs entirely in quality of tone from the Trombones though
it is so often employed in combination with these instruments,
usually acting as a Double Bass to the brass group, *i.e.* doubling
the Bass Trombone, which has the bass of the harmony, an octave
below. Among great orchestral composers Sibelius, perhaps, is most
conscious of the individuality of the Tuba as may be seen from a
study of his scores.

It may be a help to the reader in learning the sounds of the
instruments to give a few examples of solo passages in well-known
works so that he may look out for them when he hears these works
performed. Here are some, taken at random :

FLUTE.
    BACH—Suite in B minor for Flute and Strings.
       ,,   Brandenburg Concertos Nos. 2, 4, 5.
    MOZART—Magic Flute, Finales of 1st and 2nd Acts.
    BEETHOVEN—Symphony No. 3, last movement (Min. Score page 146.
          bar, 92).
       ,,   Overture Leonora No. 3 (Min. Score page 34, bar 328).
    MENDELSSOHN—Italian Symphony, last movement (Min. Score page 80).
    TSCHAIKOWSKY—Piano Concerto in B flat minor, Andantino (Min. Score
          page 108).
    DEBUSSY—L'aprés midi d'un Faune, opening.
    DELIUS—Brigg Fair, opening.

OBOE.
    BEETHOVEN—Symphony No. 6, Scherzo (Min. Score page 96, bar 91).
    SCHUBERT—Symphony in C major, opening of Andante (Min. Score
          page 92, bar 8).
    BRAHMS—Violin Concerto, opening of 2nd movement (Min. Score page
          74, bar 3).
    WAGNER—Siegfried Idyll (Min. Score page 11, bar 91).
    MAHLER—Song of the Earth, opening of 2nd movement.
    DELIUS—Brigg Fair, entry of the Theme.

COR ANGLAIS.
    BERLIOZ—Carnaval Romain (Min. Score page 3, bar 21).
       ,,   Fantastic Symphony, Adagio.
    WAGNER—Tristan and Isolde, opening of 3rd Act.
    DVORAK—New World Symphony, 2nd movement.
    FRANCK—Symphony in D, 2nd movement (Min. Score page 62, bar 16).
    DELIUS—Dance Rhapsody No. 1, opening.

CLARINET.
    Mozart—Clarinet Concerto.
      ,,   Clarinet Quintet.
      ,,   Symphony in E flat, Trio of Minuet (Min. Score page 45, bar 45).
    Beethoven—Symphony No. 4, 2nd movement (Min. Score page 47, bar 36).
      ,,   Symphony No. 6, 1st movement (Min. Score page 105, bar 1).
    Weber—Der Freischütz, Overture, low notes near end of Introduction (Min. Score page 3, bar 25).
      ,,   Der Freischütz, Overture, 2nd subject (Min. Score page 12, bar 64).
      ,,   Oberon, Overture, 2nd subject (Min. Score page 12, bar 64).
    Tschaikowsky—Low notes at the beginning of Symphony No. 5 (Min. Score page 1).
               There are many Clarinet solos in his works.
    Sibelius—Symphony No. 1, opening.
    Prokofieff—Peter and the Wolf, " The Cat " (Min. Score page 12).

BASS CLARINET.
    Wagner—Tristan and Isolde, " King Mark's Song " in 2nd Act.
    Tschaikowsky—Nutcracker Suite, " Danse de la Fée Dragée " (Min. Score page 34).
    Delius—Paris (Full Score page 5).
    Stravinsky—Petrouchka, Moor Scene, Figure 65 (Score p. 79).

BASSOON.
    Beethoven—Violin Concerto, last movement (Min. Score page 77, bar 134).
      ,,   Symphony No. 4, last movement (Min. Score page 110, bar 184).
      ,,   Symphony No. 5, 2nd movement, piu mosso (Min. Score page 49, bar 205).
    Tschaikowsky—Symphony No. 6, opening.
      ,,   Symphony No. 6, last movement (Min. Score page 214, bar 30).
    Rimsky-Korsakoff—Scheherazade, beginning of section in B minor, accompanied by held chords on divided Double Basses (Min. Score page 43)
    Dukas—L'Apprenti Sorcier, Figure 7.
    Moussorgsky-Ravel—Pictures from an Exhibition, " Il Vecchio Castello " (Min. Score page 23).
    Elgar—Cockaigne Overture (Min. Score page 37).
    Stravinsky—Le Sacre du Printemps, opening (extreme high notes).
    Ireland—A London Overture (Min. Score page 67).

DOUBLE BASSOON.
    Solos for this instrument are very rare, but a well-known example comes from the " Beauty and the Beast " number from Ravel's Mother Goose Suite. Another example for a Double Bassoon solo is the last movement of Mahler's Symphony No. 9 (Score page 167)

HORN.

BACH—Quoniam from the Mass in B minor.
BEETHOVEN—Fidelio, Overture, opening (Min. Score page 8, bar 49).
,,   Trios of Scherzos of Symphony No. 3 and No. 8 (Min Score page 112 bar 166, and page 63, bar 44).
,,   Choral Symphony, Adagio, important solo of the 4th Horn (Min. Score, page 137, bar 82).
WEBER—Der Freischütz, Overture, Introduction (Min. Score page 2, bar 10).
,,   Oberon, Overture, opening.
MENDELSSOHN—Nocturne from Midsummer Night's Dream, Horn quartet.
TSCHAIKOWSKY—Symphony No. 5, Andante (Min. Score page 69).
RICHARD STRAUSS—Till Eulenspiegel, beginning of Allegro.
MAHLER—Corno obbligato in Scherzo of Symphony No. 5.
,,   Opening of Symphony No. 3 with 8 Horns playing in unison.
DELIUS—Appalachia, opening.
VAUGHAN WILLIAMS—Pastoral Symphony, opening and letter L.
Many examples of passages for 4 Horns in unison are to be found in the works of modern composers, particularly, perhaps, Strauss, Mahler and Elgar, whose Horn writing is often of a virtuoso character.

MUTED HORN.

BEETHOVEN—Symphony No. 6, end of last movement (Min. Score page 147, bar 260).
,,   Violin Concerto, 2nd movement (Min. Score page 68, bar 86).
TSCHAIKOWSKY—Hamlet, Lento lugubre.
STRAVINSKY—Petrouchka, closing scene, 4 Muted Horns (Full Score page 155).
Numerous examples will be found in modern works by such composers as Vaughan Williams, Bax, Walton, Milhaud, Honneger, Prokofieff, etc.

TRUMPET.

HANDEL—" Let the Bright Seraphim," from Samson, Trumpet obbligato.
HAYDN—Trumpet Concerto.
BACH—Brandenburg Concerto No. 2.
BEETHOVEN—Overture Leonora No. 3, Trumpet call behind the scenes (Min. Score page 30).
WAGNER—The Ring, Sword Motive,.
,,   Prelude to Parsifal, beginning at 9th bar (Min. Score page 3).
MOUSSORGSKY-RAVEL—Pictures from an Exhibition, No. 1 " Promenade ".
VAUGHAN WILLIAMS—Pastoral Symphony, 2nd Movement, 7th bar after letter F.
,,   ,,   Pastoral Symphony, 3rd movement, Scherzo, 4 bars before letter E.
MAHLER—Symphony No. 9, 3rd movement (Full Score page 134).
DELIUS—Brigg Fair, with octaves (Full Score page 27, Min. Score page 29).
BENJAMIN BRITTEN—Sinfonia da Requiem, 2nd movement (Min. Score page 31).

Trumpet solos are comparatively rare, but many fanfare-like passages are to be found in scores of all kinds, either for solo Trumpet or Trumpets in two or three parts, *e.g.* in Tschaikowsky's Capriccio Italien, Rimsky-Korsakov's Coq d'Or and Capriccio Espagnole, Strauss's Heldenleben, not to mention the colossal "Tuba Mirum" from Berlioz's Requiem.

MUTED TRUMPET.

WAGNER—Passages from Siegfried (Scenes of Mime).
   „   Passages from Meistersinger (Scenes of Beckmesser).
Since his time practically no composer has failed to use this effect. The following are a few examples of works in which muted Trumpets appear prominently :—

DEBUSSY—Fêtes from 3 Nocturnes, 3 muted Trumpets in harmony (Min. Score page 42).

STRAUSS—Till Eulenspiegel (Full Score page 19).
   „   Don Quixote (Full Score page 8).

RAVEL—Bolero (Full Score page 11).

MOUSSORGSKY-RAVEL—Pictures from an Exhibition No. 6 (Min. Score page 67).

STRAVINSKY—Le Sacre du Printemps (Min. Score page 12).

TROMBONE.

Solos are rare because of the nature of the instrument, which is not well suited to smooth cantabile style. The three Trombones are most often used in harmony with the rest of the Brass. The following are some examples of solo or prominent Trombone passages :—

MOZART—Don Giovanni, 2nd Act, Scene of the Commendatore.
   „   Requiem, Tuba Mirum.

SCHUMANN—Symphony No. 3 in E flat (Rhenish) 4th movement.

BERLIOZ—Many passages in his works, notably the Carnaval Romain Overture (Min. Score page 40, bar 315).

WAGNER—Tannhäuser, Overture (Min. Score page 3, bar 37).
   „   Lohengrin, Prelude to Act 3 (Min. Score page 20, bar 32).
   „   The Ride of the Valkyries (Min. Score page 5, bar 12).

TSCHAIKOWSKY—Symphony No. 4, opening (Min. Score pages 1–2, bar 5).
   „   Symphony No. 6, quiet passage for Trombones and Tuba in Finale (Min. Score page 230).

Much effective Trombone writing in most of his works, also in those of Rimsky-Korsakoff and the Russian School in general.

MAHLER—Song of the Earth, 4th movement, Figure 12.
   „   Symphony No. 3, 1st movement, long solo on Trombone (Score pages 50–51).

ELGAR—Cockaigne, Overture (Min. Score page 27).
   „   Violin Concerto, 2nd movement, 3rd bar after Figure 49 (Min. Score page 47).

HOLST—The Perfect Fool, opening of ballet music.

RAVEL—Bolero, 2 bars after Figure 10.

STRAUSS—Le Bourgeois Gentilhomme, Scene of the Fencing Master.

MUTED TROMBONE.

ELGAR—Symphony No. 1 in A flat (near the end of the slow movement) (Min. Score page 120).

STRAUSS—Salome, closing scene.

VAUGHAN WILLIAMS—Symphony in F minor, near the end of the slow movement.

„   „   Job, "Satan's Dance of Triumph" (Min. Score p. 20).

BAX—Many examples on his orchestral works. In fact there can hardly be a modern score without the use of this effect somewhere or other.

TUBA.

WAGNER—Faust Overture, opening.

„   Siegfried and the Dragon (Siegfried).

MOUSSORGSKY-RAVEL—Pictures from an Exhibition, Bydlo (Min. Score page 45).

STRAUSS—Don Quixote, Tenor and Bass Tuba prominent.

STRAVINSKY—Petrouchka, "The Bear Walking on His Hind Legs," 2 bars after figure 100 (Score page 115).

CHAPTER VII. PLAYING FROM SCORE.

REFERENCE has been made in these pages to playing from score on the piano. It may therefore be not out of place to give a few hints on this subject. Naturally, a great deal depends on the pianistic skill of the player but, granted average ability and some skill in ordinary sight-reading, fair results may be obtained at any rate with music of which the texture is comparatively simple and the pace not too quick. Apart from the agility of eye and hand required in quick movements there is the extreme frequency of turning over the page.

The best results can be got out of score-reading on two pianos, one player taking Strings and the other Wind and Brass, and a really good full version of the score can be given by two skilled players in this way provided they each have someone to turn over for them. But the majority will have to plough a lonely furrow, and though nothing but practice will bring facility, a few hints may be found useful.

(1) It is above all necessary to keep cool, and not to allow one-self to be bewildered by what appears at first sight to be a maze of notes. Before beginning to play, the score should be quietly examined so that essential parts may be disentangled from those which are mere filling-up and unison and octave doublings which may give apparent complexity to the look of the score by reason of different clefs and transpositions may be discerned. Most passages in the simpler classics will be found to be based on part-writing in three or four parts. Some knowledge of harmony is a great advantage as melody and bass usually give the clue to the harmony, but the reader who has not this knowledge need not be deterred though his progress may be relatively rather slow.

(2) Whatever else is lacking, apart from the principal melodic line, the bass must be played, otherwise the whole structure lacks foundation. When the Double Basses are playing, the Bass should be played in octaves where possible, but if this prevents the inclusion of important inner parts a single-line Bass will have to suffice.

(3) In a passage consisting of block-chords, do not try to play the

chords exactly as they are laid out for the orchestra, but play it in such a way that the chords lie well under the hand. This is one of the cases in which a knowledge of conventional harmony is very useful.

(4) Be prepared to cross left hand over right and *vice versa* in order to avoid awkward jumping about of the hands, which soon leads to flurry and confusion.

(5) Do not think it necessary to reproduce octave-doublings of melodic lines if this results in too much thinness of harmony.

(6) In contrapuntal passages it will often be found that the sense of the passage and its harmonic basis can be sufficiently given if the two outside parts only are played, with perhaps an occasional suggestion of inner parts to keep up the feeling of movement, but do not get into the lazy habit of always playing practically nothing but the 1st Violin and bass part and calling it score-reading.

(7) Leave nothing out that can be comfortably put in, and be very honest with yourself about the viola parts and the parts for transposing instruments. Do not slur them over or " take them as read " when they are within easy reach.

(8) Suppose there is an important accompaniment figure going on in the 2nd Violins, Violas or Clarinets of an arpeggio-like nature. It may not always be possible to reproduce its exact shape or to play it at the pitch of the original. Be prepared to alter it a little here and there and if necessary to pass it from hand to hand in order to preserve the smooth movement of melody and bass. Remember that your aim is to give a sketch of the work, not a detailed and perfect performance.

(9) Rapid repeated notes are easy on stringed instruments and frequently occur in orchestral music. The piano is not well suited to them and on it they should be represented by broken octaves, *e.g.*

1st and 2nd Violins

Piano

(10) Tremolo chords on the Strings are similarly represented, thus :

Drum rolls are also represented by broken octaves.

(11) Compare published piano arrangements of works with the full scores. This will teach you more about piano-reduction than anything else can do.

(12) Beginners are sometimes advised to start by reading string quartets at the piano. This is not sound advice. No well-written quartet lends itself to piano transcription because each of the four strands of the texture is important as it stands and is incapable of alteration without complete ruina-tion to the effect. Chamber music is pure music composed of interweaving lines. Orchestral music from Haydn onwards is music of effect and is composed of contrasted masses of sound. Its details can therefore be regarded as of secondary importance to the general effect at all events in the matter of representation in black-and-white on the piano. A start should be made with the slow movements of symphonies by Haydn and Mozart, proceeding through those of Beethoven to more complex scores as experience is gained.

CHAPTER VIII. ORCHESTRATION.

THE art of orchestration is a very complicated and intricate one and it will only be possible here to give the merest outline of what the scoring of a piece of music really involves. When a composer writes for the piano he is able even if he is only a mediocre pianist himself, to try over passages as he goes along and to alter and correct them accordingly, but when he is writing for orchestra he is dependent solely on his inner ear. He cannot have an orchestra on tap so to speak, so that he can try over a doubtful bar here and there, and though he has probably started by writing a short score of the work so that he can gain an idea of its effect on the piano in black and white, the realisation of the music as it will sound in its orchestral dress has to be purely imaginary. No wonder then that even the most experienced writers for the orchestra are on tenterhooks before the first rehearsal of a new work. Will the Flute come through here, will the Horns be too prominent there, will the Clarinet be able to manage that tricky looking passage on page 100, will that big climax sound well-balanced and rich in sonority. In fact, after a sleepless night of trepidation he wonders if *anything* will sound right ! The painter can see his creation grow under his hands, the sculptor can model and remodel his clay from which the bronze is to be cast or the marble cut, the writer can read and gauge his effects as he writes, but the orchestral composer can only hear the result of his work when it is finished and it will probably be too late to alter anything before the first performance which quite likely will follow the rehearsal at an interval of only a few hours. Yet it is rare that an experienced orchestral composer makes bad mistakes. A passage may not sound exactly as he imagined it, but it will " come off " in performance and the whole effect of the work from an orchestral point of view will be satisfactory. In fact it is not unknown for score parts actually to be printed and thus made irrevocable before the composer has had a chance of hearing it.

How is it done ?

First of all our composer must have heard countless orchestral works, and have studied many scores of all styles and periods so that the sound of an orchestra has bitten right into his inner consciousness, and normal technical devices, the bread and butter of orchestration, are so familiar as to be taken for granted.

Secondly, he must have made himself acquainted with the character and capabilities of all the instruments he uses. This does not mean that he needs to be able to play any of them, indeed, some very accomplished orchestral composers cannot play a note on any instrument that they write for. Actually, a little ability to play an instrument may be a disadvantage for he may feel inhibited in writing for that instrument by his own lack of technical skill upon it, but it is manifestly an advantage to be a good or moderately good performer on as many of the instruments as possible. Elgar played the Violin, Bassoon and Trombone as well as the Piano and Organ ; on the other hand Berlioz could play no instrument at all, not even the piano, unless one counts his slight first hand knowledge of the Guitar which cannot have been of much use to him as an orchestral composer. The best training ground is, of course, the orchestra itself, and it is more the fact of having experience of the orchestra from the inside that is valuable than the actual ability to play an instrument. There is no doubt, however, that some people have an inborn flair for the orchestra which is a natural gift, and those who have it to a marked degree will find their own way of developing their powers whether they have practical opportunities, such as playing in an orchestra, or not. The fact remains that, however it is obtained, a knowledge of the possibilities and limitations of instruments is absolutely essential to the composer, and this knowledge continues to grow and accumulate all through his career.

Thirdly, he must acquire a sense of balance. Not only do instruments have different tone-colours, but they vary very much in strength and power. The most powerful instrument in the orchestra is the Trombone ; the weakest, the Flute on its bottom notes. A note may be written and marked fortissimo for Trombone and the same note marked fortissimo for the Flute, but the difference measured in the decibels of the scientist would be overwhelming. In modern scores where niceties of balance are more carefully put down on paper than they were in classical times, and where infinitely more subtle nuances of tone are aimed at, it is common to find different degrees of loudness indicated for different instruments or groups of instruments in order to obtain satisfactory balance and to ensure sufficient prominence for important lines in the texture and sufficient effacement for the background. Doubling of several instruments in unison or octaves is also often used to ensure good balance, and to bring important melodies into sufficient prominence.

Fourthly, the composer must have a good sense of contrast and variety so as to avoid too long a continuance of one sort of tone-colour. Among the great composers Schumann was weakest in this respect. He kept his instruments going too long at a time and his orchestration is therefore more monotonous and heavy as a general rule than one would like. A notable exception to this is found in his Piano Concerto, which sounds clear and is well varied in tone-colour throughout. The admirers of Brahms stoutly defend his orchestration, while others find it dull and too austere, not because, like Schumann, of too unvarying a texture but because his attitude to tone-colour was severe and strait-laced in its avoidance of a direct appeal to the senses. One never feels that Brahms revelled in orchestral sound for its own sake as, for instance, Berlioz, Wagner, Strauss and Rimsky-Korsakoff did, in fact one gets the impression that he " orchestrated " his works, whereas the others directly conceived theirs for the orchestra, which is a very different matter.

Fifthly, the harmony must be disposed in such a way that it achieves fullness without thickness and also avoids sounding " all top and bottom ". To get intriguing effects from a few instruments is easy, but the real test of an orchestrator lies in his ability to write a fully scored passage so that it sounds well balanced and imposing and yet brilliant and striking.

Sixthly, the interest of the players should be aroused by writing parts which are agreeable and pleasant to play. There always has to be some dull filling-in to be done, but the wise composer sees to it that the dull patches are compensated for by more interesting ones in other parts of the work.

Seventhly, the composer may have to take into consideration the idiosyncracies of some particular orchestra for which the work is primarily written. For instance there may be a particularly brilliant 1st Flute in it, the 2nd Bassoon may be somewhat lacking in technique, the Brass section may be specially uniform in tone and fine in its blend, or the Strings not very numerous. Such things will be in the mind of the composer as he works and his ideas will adapt themselves accordingly, but of course these conditions only apply to a work commissioned for a special purpose.

There are many other technical considerations also to be taken into account, but the above will give the reader some idea of the complexity of the task of writing orchestral music. They also apply to the matter of the arrangement for orchestra of music originally written for some other medium, often the piano. The ballets " Sylphides " " Carnaval " and " Apparitions " provide examples of this. In this type of work the music has not only to be orchestrated but its texture has to be re-arranged so as to be orchestral instead of pianistic in character. The effect of the sustaining pedal for instance has to be taken into account and amplifications and decorations have to be added to give the music the colour and interest that the larger medium calls for. Arrangement is a derivative art of course, but it is one that calls for much good taste and skill. A splendid example is Ravel's orchestration of Moussorgsky's " Pictures from an Exhibition ". Ravel also arranged much of his own music for orchestra, having originally written it for piano, for instance, the Suite " Le Tombeau de Couperin ", " Pavane pour une infante défunte " and the Suite " Ma Mère L'Oye ". Brahms, too, arranged his Variations on a theme of Haydn, originally written for two pianos, for orchestra.

CHAPTER IX.

THE INSTRUMENTS OF THE ORCHESTRA BRIEFLY CONSIDERED.

THE instruments are taken in the order in which they appear in a score.

FLUTE.

Compass 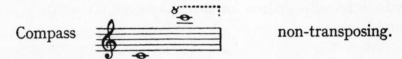 non-transposing.

Tone. Rich and full but easily obscured in the lowest octave. Pure and limpid above this.

Normal use. Doubling 1st Violins or the other Woodwind at the octave above. Used also for rapid decorative passages. In solo work it has an antique pagan character in its medium register.

PICCOLO.

Compass 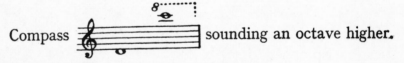 sounding an octave higher.

Not much used in bottom octave.

Tone. Shrill and acute in high registers.

Normal use. Doubling Flutes at the octave above in fortissimo passages for full orchestra. Used quietly it adds great brightness and piquancy especially in staccato work.

OBOE.

Compass  non-transposing.

The extreme high and low notes are rarely used. Tone very characteristic. Plaintive and reedy. Pastoral in character, but in staccato work playful or even spiteful at times.

Normal use. Solo passages, often very short, but can draw a fine long expressive line. Capable of considerable execution, but not comparable in this respect with Flute and Clarinet.

COR ANGLAIS.

Compass 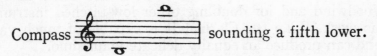 sounding a fifth lower.

Tone. Very characteristic. Hollow and woody on lowest notes. Tragic and expressive in medium register. Can be distinguished from the Oboe by its rounder, more throaty tone.

Normal use. Chiefly used for solo work ; but often doubles Violas and/or 'Cellos in melodic passages. Its telling tone makes it unfit for unobtrusive filling-in parts. It usually has something definite and important to say.

CLARINET.

Compass (written)  sounding when in B flat a tone lower, when in A a minor third lower.

Extreme high notes rarely used.

Tone. Very rich and characteristic in bottom octave (known as the " chalumeau "). Cool and clear in medium register, shrill on the top notes. Capable of more variety of loud and soft than any other wind instrument. When played very softly it can produce a mere wisp of sound.

Normal use. Very adaptable. Excellent for solo work. Passages in thirds and sixths for two Clarinets are frequently used and are very effective. Very useful for filling-in also. Capable of rapid execution. Arpeggio passages very effective and much used, sometimes at great speed.

BASS CLARINET.

Compass (written)  sounding when in B flat a major ninth lower, when in A a minor tenth lower.

Alternative notation is in the Bass clef, in which case the transposition is a tone and a minor third lower for the B flat and A instrument respectively. The Bass Clarinet in A is now obsolete.

Tone. Very velvety and unique in quality in the lowest octave. Above that the tone is something between that of a 'Cello and a Saxophone. The top notes are very rarely used.

Normal use. Generally employed for the effect of its low notes. Quite often used for solo passages, but is also useful as a bass to the Woodwind and for doubling other low-pitched instruments in melodic work. Like the Clarinet it is capable of much variety of tone and can produce an equally delicate pianissimo.

BASSOON.

Compass  non-transposing.

Tone. Rich and deep in bottom register. Expressive and 'Cello-like in medium register. High notes rather thin and querulous.

Normal use. Of the utmost value in the orchestra. It can be a good soloist, double melodies an octave below Violins or the higher Woodwind instruments, act as bass to the Woodwind group or take the bass line with the Double Basses when the 'Cellos are required for melodic work. Blends admirably with Horns, Clarinets and Strings, and is of great use in filling-in harmony notes in the tenor register, quietly and unobtrusively. It is capable of considerable execution and its dry staccato is sometimes exploited for its humorous quality.

DOUBLE BASSOON.

Compass 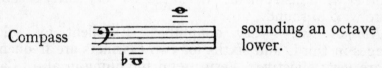 sounding an octave lower.

Tone. Very gruff and powerful on lowest notes.

Normal use. Reinforcing the Double Basses in fully scored passages.

HORN.

Compass (Valve Horn)  Horn in F, sounds a fifth lower.

For other transpositions see Chapter III.

Tone. Round and rich in medium register. Extreme high notes rather rare. Bottom notes (chiefly used by 2nd and 4th

Horns) growly, but useful for long held notes. The tone is expressive and poetic in quiet solos, rough and penetrating in fortissimo.

Normal use. Filling in, holding long notes, some solo work. Passages for four Horns in unison are effective and frequently used in modern music since Wagner. Blends well with Bassoons and Clarinets and reinforces 'Cellos in melodic passages admirably. The Horn quartet makes a rich middle for the orchestra. Muted and hand-stopped effects are common in modern scores.

TRUMPET.

Compass
(Valve Trumpet)

In C (non-transposing). Also in B flat and A, transposition the same as for Clarinets.

For other transpositions see Chapter III.

Tone. Very rich and penetrating in forte and fortissimo ; quiet tone is equally noble and imposing except on very high notes which are rather screamy but highly exciting.

Normal use. Occasional solo passages, but not suitable for anything of a romantic character as such melodies become vulgarised on the Trumpet. Capable of considerable execution, but most suited to fanfare-like passages, crisp chord-playing with Trombones, or sustained work. Always makes its presence felt and is therefore unsuitable for unobtrusive filling-in. Rapid repetition of notes (double or triple tonguing) is very effective.

When muted and played softly it changes its character, producing a quiet far-away tone slightly nasal and devoid of all the martial pomp associated with the normal sounds. When muted and played loudly the nasal character is much amplified and the tone is harsh and very penetrating.

TENOR TROMBONE.

Compass

non-transposing.

Tone. Similar to that of the Trumpet, taking differences of pitch into account. Blend of Trombones and Trumpets is therefore perfect.

Normal use. Two Tenor Trombones and Bass Trombone are used as a group in three-part harmony and are capable of all degrees of force from *ppp* to *fff*. Solo-work is rather rare, but the three Trombones are often used in unison for melodies of a grand and impressive type. When played softly they blend admirably with the Horns. Effective chord-spacing for Trombones plays a very important part in the effectiveness of passages for full orchestra. Crisp chords produce a fine crackling effect, while sustained work has a nobility unsurpassed in the orchestra, especially if the tone is unforced.

Muted Trombone effects are even more nasal in tone than those of muted Trumpets.

BASS TROMBONE.

Compass  non-transposing.

Tone. Similar to Tenor Trombone, but if anything it is more powerful and its low notes are definitely of better quality than those of the tenor instrument.

Normal use. Acts as bass to the Brass section and works in three-part harmony with the Tenor Trombones.

BASS TUBA.

Compass  non-transposing.

Notes above the Bass staff are rarely used.

Tone. Round and full, never achieves like the Trombones a cutting edge.

Normal use. Doubles the Bass Trombone at the octave below, and sometimes makes true four-part harmony with the Trombones. Reinforces important bass lines, and is rarely used as a solo instrument, and then only for some special dramatic effect as a rule.

TIMPANI.

When two Drums are used they have the following compasses :

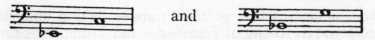

When three are employed the extra Drum lies between the two given above, viz :

" Machine-drums " are also used in some orchestras (see Chapter IV).

Tone. Resonant, and gives true pitch especially on the medium and higher notes. Capable of producing all shades of tone from *ppp* to *fff* both in single notes and rolls.

Normal use. Marking the rhythm, playing long or short rolls, crescendo or diminuendo or sustained at equal pressure. Adds great power to the full orchestra, but is capable of very delicate effects. A real musical instrument. The timpanist is a very important member of the orchestra.

Other Percussion instruments.

These give notes of indeterminate pitch, those in most common use being Bass Drum, Cymbals, Triangle, Tambourine and Side Drum. Others less frequently used are Gong, Jingles, Castanets, Tenor Drum, Chinese Block, etc.

Normal use. To mark the rhythm, add weight to climaxes, introduce local colour and dramatic effects. These instruments are not only used loudly, but are all capable of artistic and delicate use.

THE GLOCKENSPIEL.

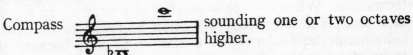

Compass — sounding one or two octaves higher.

Tone. Clear and bell-like, produced by striking resonant little metal bars.

Normal use. Isolated notes, simple melodic figures, and bell-like passages.

THE XYLOPHONE.

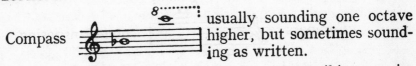

Compass — usually sounding one octave higher, but sometimes sounding as written.

Tone. Dry and " chippy ". It is produced by striking a series of wooden bars.

Normal use. Very agile, effective in very rapidly repeated notes, combines well with pizzicato strings. Hard, expressionless and brilliant.

THE CELESTA.

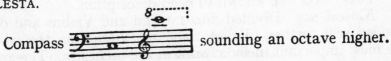

Compass — sounding an octave higher.

This instrument has a keyboard like a piano, the tone being produced by hammers striking steel bars. Its part is written on two staves like piano-music.

Tone. Clearer and rounder than that of the Glockenspiel.

Normal use. Solo-work of very light and airy character. capable of considerable execution, the notes have some sustaining power. Used as a charming colour-effect.

THE HARP.

Compass  non-transposing.

The Harp has a special technique, the pitch of the notes being altered chromatically by means of pedals.

Tone. Too well known to need description. Its part is written on two staves like piano music.

Normal use. Adding richness to the orchestral ensemble by means of arpeggios, chords and so on. Often used to accompany solo wind or stringed instruments. Glissandi are often used, also harmonics. When a piece is written in a very sharp key such as B or F sharp the Harp part will often be found to be written in the enharmonic equivalent, *i.e.* C flat or G flat, because its special technique is more favourable to remote flat keys than remote sharp ones. Those who wish to discover exactly how the Harp works must consult a text-book of orchestration. It is too complicated to go into in detail here.

THE VIOLIN.

Compass  non-transposing.

A few higher notes can be obtained as harmonics.

Open strings  1st string.
2nd string.
3rd string.
4th string.

Tone. Too well known to need description.

Normal use. Divided into 1st and 2nd Violins and often subdivided still further (divisi). The 1st Violins on the whole carry the most important melodic work in the orchestra. The 2nd Violins provide an inner part or double the 1st Violins in unison or at the octave below. Double stops, tremolos and pizzicato are frequent devices in the orchestra. The mute is often used. Much brilliance is often imparted to a passage for full orchestra by rapid running passages for the Violins while Brass and Woodwind provide the chief thematic interest, but the 1st Violins are primarily melodic.

THE VIOLA.

Compass

Higher notes *can* be obtained especially by the use of harmonics.

Open strings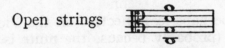

Tone. Very characteristic in the bottom octave (C string), powerful and becoming rather reedy as it ascends.

Normal use. Supplies inner parts in alto and tenor register, frequently called upon to play double stops and chords, while tremolo and pizzicato are common. Sometimes used melodically, especially when doubling the Violins at the lower octave. Not infrequently a melody is written in three octaves for 1st and 2nd Violins and Violas. In the early classics the Viola part often doubles the bass line in unison or at the octave above because Viola players could not then be entrusted with much independent work owing to their lack of technique.

Mutes are very effective on the Violas. Viola parts are frequently divided into two or more parts (divisi) especially in modern works.

THE VIOLONCELLO.

Compass  non-transposing

Higher notes may appear in solo 'Cello parts both as ordinary and harmonic notes.

Open strings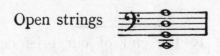

Tone. Rich, full and powerful in lowest register. Middle notes less powerful (the tone of the two middle strings of all stringed instruments is less powerful than that of the outside ones) but of pleasing musical quality. The top string is very expressive and penetrating and its quality will no doubt be familiar to readers.

Normal use. Plays the bass line with or without the Double Basses. Also plays melodies and counter melodies in the tenor register, either doubled in unison by other instruments of like pitch or alone. Combines well in unison with Violas, Horns, Clarinets, Bassoons and Cor Anglais. Violoncello parts, like those of the other strings, are frequently divided nowadays into two or more parts (divisi). The pizzicato is resonant and is much used. Double stops, chords, tremolos and so on are also frequently to be met with.

The mute is perhaps less effective on the Violoncello than on the higher strings (probably because the mute is often not heavy enough), but it is used when the other Strings are muted, though in early classical days this was not so.

THE DOUBLE BASS.

Compass ... sounding an octave lower.

Higher notes are possible, obtained both in the ordinary way and as harmonics.

Tone. Rather gruff and dry when used alone, but when doubled an octave higher by Violoncellos or Bassoons the Double Basses give great depth and power to the bass line. They rarely come out into the open, as it were, but are extremely important nevertheless because without them the bass of the orchestra would be lamentably weak and deficient. Their pizzicato is immensely effective and resonant, having considerable duration, and is much used. Double stops and chords are extremely rare, but nowadays " divisi ", especially in octaves or fifths is of frequent occurrence. Long sustained notes in forte passages are not possible without changing the direction of the bow fairly frequently, but they are often written in scores, the players changing their bows at different times. Tremolos cannot be kept up long at great speed as they are very fatiguing.

This brings us to the end of our brief descriptions of the

instruments in ordinary use. For the sake of completeness **we** now add a few similar remarks on the rarely-used instruments.

The Bass Flute.

Compass   sounding a fourth lower.

Tone. Very rich and full in the lowest register.

Normal use. As a solo instrument. Capable, like the ordinary Flute, of much execution.

The Oboe d'amore.

Compass   sounding a minor third lower.

In the scores of Bach, parts for this instrument are written at their true pitch, but when used in modern scores the above transposition is always employed.

Tone. Between that of the Oboe and Cor Anglais. Less pungent than the Oboe but not so throaty and heavy as the Cor Anglais.

Normal use. As a solo instrument.

The Heckelphone.

Compass   sounding an octave lower.

Tone. Very reedy and sinister in its low register.

Normal use. As a solo instrument and as a bass to the Oboe-Cor Anglais group.

The Clarinet in E flat.

Compass   sounding a minor third higher.

Tone. Similar to the ordinary Clarinet in its lower registers. Upper notes shrill and penetrating.

Normal use. Reinforces the Flutes in fully scored passages.

Also used as a solo instrument. A regular constituent of the Military Band.

THE BASSET HORN (Corno di Bassetto).

This was a Tenor Clarinet in F which was ousted early in the nineteenth century by the Bass Clarinet. Mozart made extensive use of it in " Die Zauberflöte " and also used it in his Requiem and in " Die Entführung " (Constanze's Aria). He also used the instrument in some of his chamber works for wind instruments.

Compass — sounding a fifth lower.

Tone. Rich, full, reedy and rather sombre in low and medium registers. High notes rarely used.

Normal use. Mozart used it as an *obbligato* instrument in some of his operatic works, also to aid in giving a dark and impressive character to the orchestral ensemble as in " Die Zauberflöte " and the Requiem. Its use in Mozart's scores has kept it from becoming obsolete, but examples of its employment by more recent composers are almost non-existent as far as the writer knows.

THE SAXOPHONE.

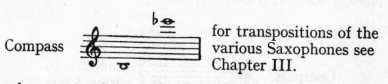

Compass — for transpositions of the various Saxophones see Chapter III.

The Saxophone most frequently used in the orchestra is the **Alto in E flat.**

Tone. No doubt all too familiar to the reader from its use in Dance bands.

Normal use. As a solo instrument. In Military Bands the Alto Saxophone in E flat and the Tenor in B flat are regularly used.

THE SARRUSOPHONE.

Compass — sounding an octave lower.

Used by some French composers instead of the Double Bassoon.

THE CORNET.

Compass 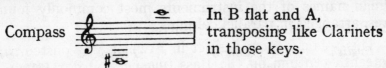 In B flat and A, transposing like Clarinets in those keys.

Tone. Similar to the trumpet but with less character and far less nobility.

Normal use. French composers of the last century favoured its use because of its agility and its tone contrasted with that of the trumpets in F, E flat and E which were then in use. Now that the smaller Trumpets in C, B flat and A are used, the Cornet is unnecessary in the orchestra. It is, of course, the mainstay of the Brass Band, and is an important member of the Military Band. Comparatively recent works in which Cornets are used are Stravinsky's " Petrouchka ", Elgar's " Cockaigne Overture " and Vaughan Williams' " London Symphony ".

THE TENOR TUBA.

Compass  In B flat, sounding a ninth lower.

Like the Bass Clarinet, its part is also sometimes written in the Bass clef in which case it sounds only a tone lower.

Tone. Round and hollow, but penetrating.

Normal use. As a solo instrument mainly, but also to reinforce the Bass Tuba line at the octave above. Only to be found in very heavily scored works such as Strauss's " Don Quixote " and " Ein Heldenleben " and Holst's " Planets ".

The following table shows the English, Italian, French and German names of the instruments most commonly found in full scores, arranged in parallel columns :

English.	*Italian.*	*French.*	*German.*
Flute	Flauto	Flûte	Flöte
Piccolo	Flauto piccolo (or Ottavino)	Petite flûte	Kleine flöte
Oboe (or Hautboy)	Oboe	Hautbois	Hoboe
English Horn (or Cor Anglais)	Corno Inglese	Cor Anglais	Englisch Horn (or Alt-hoboe)
Clarinet	Clarinetto	Clarinette	Klarinette
Bass Clarinet	Clarinetto Basso (or Clarone)	Clarinette basse	Bassklarinette
Bassoon	Fagotto	Basson	Fagott
Double Bassoon	Contrafagotto	Contrebasson	Kontrafagott
Horn	Corno	Cor	Horn
Trumpet	Tromba	Trompette	Trompete
Trombone	Trombone	Trombone	Posaune
Tuba	Tuba	Tuba	Tuba
Kettledrums (or Timpani)	Timpani	Timbales	Pauken
Bass Drum	Gran Cassa	Grosse Caisse	Grosse Trommel
Cymbals	Piatti (or Cinelli)	Cymbales	Becken
Side Drum	Tamburo militare	Tambour militaire (or Caisse claire)	Kleine Trommel
Triangle	Triangolo	Triangle	Triangel
Tambourine	Tamburino	Tambour de Basque	Tamburin (Schellentrommel)
Gong	Tam-tam	Tam-tam	Tam-tam
Tenor Drum	Tamburo rulante	Caisse roulante	Rührtrommel
Bells	Campanelle	Carillon	Glocken
Glockenspiel	Campanetta	Cloches	Glockenspiel
Xylophone	Zilafone	Xylophone	Xylophon
Harp	Arpa	Harpe	Harfe
Violin	Violino	Violon	Violine
Viola	Viola	Alto	Bratsche
Violoncello	Violoncello	Violoncelle	Violoncell
Double Bass	Contrabasso	Contrebasse	Kontrabass

The names of the instruments are usually set out in full on the first page of the score, and in abbreviated form on subsequent pages, *e.g.* Fl., Ob., Cl., Fg., Cor, etc.

BIBLIOGRAPHY

For those who wish to pursue the subjects outlined in this book in more detail, the following books are recommended :

Berlioz. *Treatise on Instrumentation* (Novello).

Widor. *The Technique of the Modern Orchestra* (Joseph Williams).

Cecil Forsyth. *Orchestration* (Macmillan).

Harold Hind and Edwin Evans (with preface by Henry J. Wood.) *The Orchestra and its Instruments* (Boosey & Hawkes).

Rimsky-Korsakoff. *Orchestration* (Edition Russe de Musique).

Frank Howes. *Full Orchestra* (Secker and Warburg).

Gordon Jacob. *Orchestral Technique* (Oxford University Press).

Also the articles written by experts on the various orchestral instruments in Grove's *Dictionary of Music and Musicians* (Macmillan).